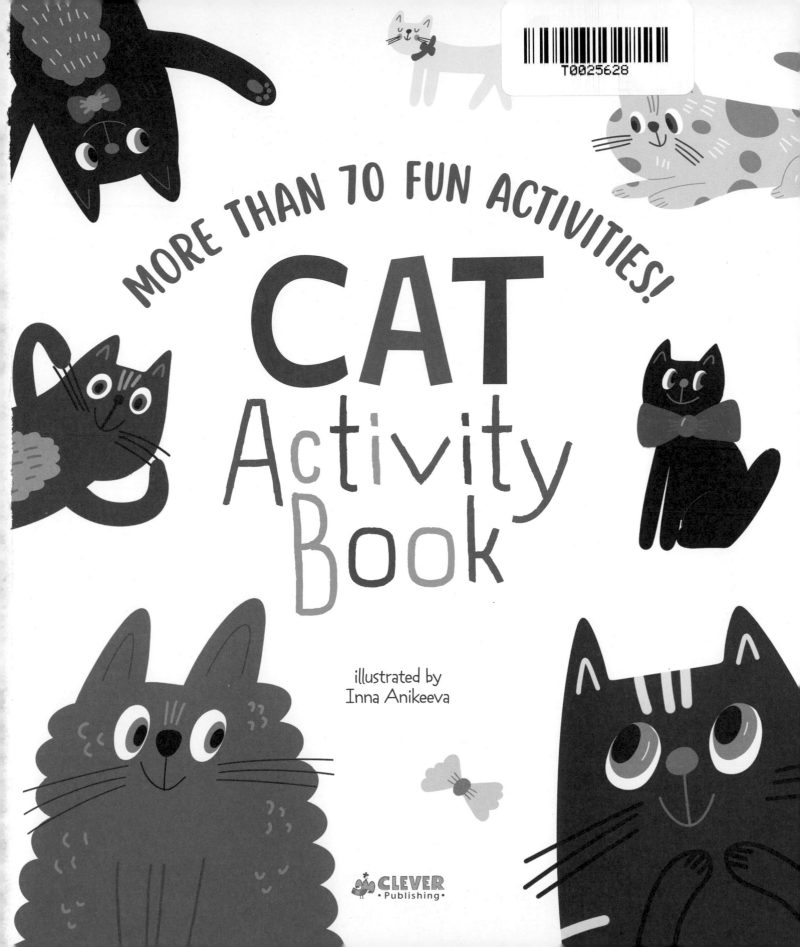

MORE THAN 70 FUN ACTIVITIES!

CAT
Activity Book

illustrated by
Inna Anikeeva

CLEVER
· Publishing ·

PICTURE PURR-FECT

Use your crayons to color this picture of Darcy the cat.

TAKE A TRIP

Len and Leo want to visit their friend Catherine.
Can you help them? Each cat must take his own path.

CATHERINE

LEO

LEN

CLIMBING HiGH

Can you help Princess find her way up the ladders to the top of the brown house?

FINISH

PRINCESS

NAP TiME

Cats can sleep up to 20 hours a day!
Help Bella find her way through the maze to get
to the cozy cat bed for a nap.

FINISH

BELLA

MEOW!

Color these cats and kittens any way you want.

Who fell asleep?

Find two identical cats.

Which cat is your favorite?

AT THE MUSEUM

Help Max through the maze to reach the stained-glass window exhibit. Then see if you can find the small pictures in the larger pictures.

FINISH

MAX

CHORUS OF CATS

Smoky wants to join his friends in the Cat Chorus.
Help him find his way through the maze, collecting
music notes as you go.

SMOKY

FINISH

THE THIEF'S HOUSE

Detective Milo knows that the thief lives in a room with a green door. Can you lead him to the thief?

A dangerous criminal lives here

CAT'S BALL

Draw a line between the matching bows.
Do you see two insects that look like bows?

Tom the cat wants to wear a bowtie. Color the bows
and Tom, too! Which bow does he want to wear?

MARBLE MAZE

Midnight, Ginger, and Chocolate are playing a marble maze game. Follow the paths to see whose marble reaches the end first.

GINGER

CHOCOLATE

MIDNIGHT

FINISH

Uh-oh! One of the cats knocked over the plant. Number the pictures 1–6 to show which came first, second, and so on. Which cat do you think made the mess?

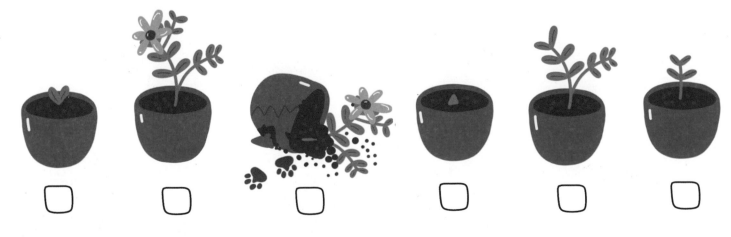

I'M SLEEPY!

Pretzel is sleepy and wants to lie down. Can you guide him through the maze to his bed?

FINISH

PRETZEL

RUN, MOUSE, RUN!

Jasper is a good hunter, but the mice are fast! Can you help Squeak the mouse get back home safely?

JASPER

SQUEAK

FINISH

LOOK AND FiND

See if you can find the objects in the box below somewhere in the picture. Use your crayons or colored pencils to color them in as you find them. Then color in the rest of the picture!

WHERE'S MY TOY?

Lily got a new toy mouse, but she lost it somewhere in the maze. Help her find it.

FINISH

LILY

MiLK MESS!

Uh-oh! Someone spilled milk all over the floor. Help Doughnut get through the mess to his friend Cookie.

DOUGHNUT

MILK

COOKIE

CAT YOGA

These cats are doing yoga! Draw lines to match the cats to their shadows. Then color in the instructor.

Find 10 differences between these two pictures.

DOMINOES

On each blank domino, every square should match the object next to it. Draw in the missing objects. The first one has been done for you. Color them in, too!

ACORN

SUN

Draw a circle around each group of 5 objects that are different. The first one has been done for you. How many groups are there?

SWEET DREAMS

It's past bedtime, but Max still wants to play! Help him reach his toys. Don't wake up Jack and Sam!

TREE HOUSE

Molly wants to visit her friend Lisa, but she needs to find her way up the tree. Can you help her?

LISA

MOLLY

TANGLE OF CATS!

Can you count the cats? Circle them as you find them.

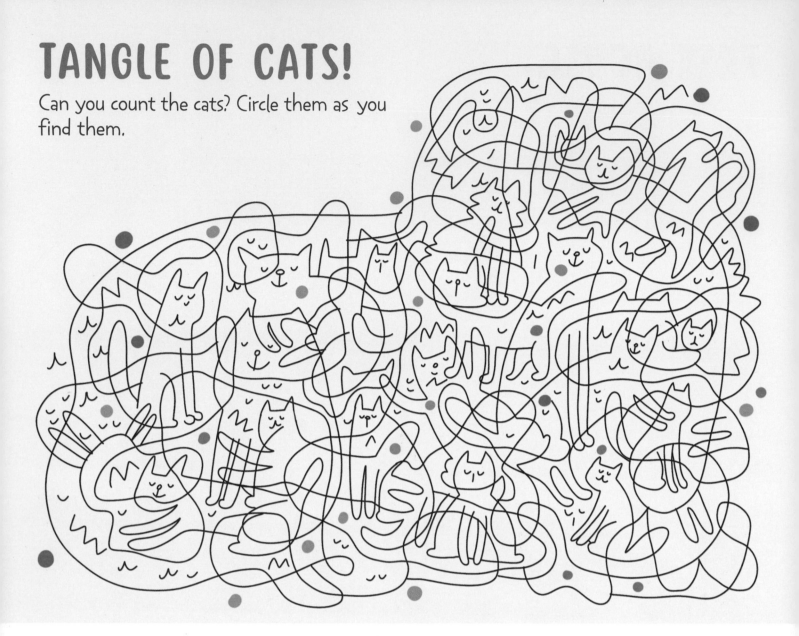

Look at the cats below. What name fits best with each cat? Write the number under each cat.

1. Butterfly
2. Prickly
3. Spots
4. Peach
5. Midnight

RACE DAY

Vroom, vroom! It's time for the race to begin. Follow each path to find out which cat finishes first.

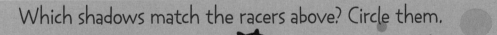

Which shadows match the racers above? Circle them.

YUM!

Oliver loves cat treats! Help collect them in order and fill his bowl using the key below.

← START

CATCHING BUTTERFLIES

Pepper is setting out to catch butterflies today. Can you help him find a way through the park? Watch out for the bear!

FINISH

PEPPER

UH-OH!

Charlie is up to his tricks again! Find the pieces that are missing from each item and circle them.

Fill in the boxes so that there is only one object of each color going across and up and down.

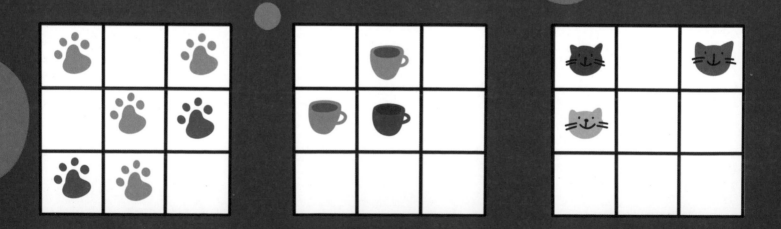

ART TiME

Finish drawing these cat faces, and then color them in. Then try drawing your own in the box below!

ROAD TRIP

Tina is meeting her friends for a road trip, but she needs to pick up a few things first. Help her collect the items.

FINISH

TINA

WHOSE COLLAR?

The kittens each have a new collar!
Follow the paths to see whose collar is whose.

CATS EVERYWHERE!

There are 25 cats hidden in this picture. Can you find them all?

FRIENDS

Simon wants to visit his friend Sam. Can you help him find his way across the water?

SAM

SIMON

AT THE BEACH

Peanut wants to sunbathe next to her friend Cathy. Find the correct path through the sand to help her get there.

CATHY

PEANUT

SECRET PLACE

Caramel likes to sleep all the way at the top of the bookshelf!
Can you help her get up there?
Be careful not to knock anything down!

FINISH

CARAMEL

WHO'S THERE?

Use the key below to color in the squares to find out who's hiding in the picture.

● 1 ○ 2 ● 3 ● 4 ● 5

5	5	5	5	5	5	5	5	5	5	5	5	5	5	5	5	5	5	2	5	5	5	5	5	5	5	5	5	5	5
5	2	5	5	5	5	5	5	5	5	5	5	5	5	5	5	5	5	5	5	5	5	5	5	5	5	5	2	5	5
5	5	5	5	5	3	3	3	3	3	3	3	3	3	3	3	3	3	3	3	3	5	2	2	2	2	5
5	5	5	5	5	5	5	5	5	5	5	5	5	3	5	5	5	5	5	5	5	5	2	2	2	2	5
5	5	5	5	5	5	5	5	5	5	5	4	4	4	4	4	4	5	5	5	2	5	5	5	5	2	5	4
5	5	5	2	5	5	5	5	5	1	1	4	4	4	1	1	4	4	5	5	5	5	5	5	5	5	4	4
5	5	2	2	2	5	5	5	1	1	1	4	4	1	1	1	4	4	4	5	5	5	5	5	5	4	4	4
5	2	2	2	2	5	5	1	1	1	2	4	4	1	1	2	4	4	4	5	5	5	5	4	4	4	4
5	5	2	2	5	5	1	1	1	1	2	4	4	1	1	1	4	4	4	4	4	4	4	4	4	4	4
5	5	5	5	5	5	1	1	1	1	1	4	4	3	3	3	4	4	4	3	3	3	3	3	4	4	4
5	5	5	5	5	3	3	3	3	3	4	4	4	4	4	4	4	4	5	5	5	5	5	3	4	4
5	5	5	5	5	5	4	4	4	4	4	4	4	4	4	4	4	5	5	5	5	5	5	3	4
2	5	5	5	5	5	3	3	3	3	3	3	3	3	3	3	5	5	5	5	5	5	2	5	5	3
5	5	5	5	5	5	5	5	3	5	5	5	5	5	5	5	3	5	5	5	5	2	2	2	5	5	5
5	5	5	5	2	5	3	5	5	3	5	5	5	5	5	5	3	5	5	3	5	5	2	2	2	2	5
5	5	5	5	5	5	3	3	3	3	3	3	3	3	3	3	3	3	3	5	5	5	5	2	5	5	5
2	5	5	5	5	5	5	5	5	5	5	5	5	5	5	5	5	5	5	5	5	5	5	5	5	5	2

Uh-oh! Someone took some sausages from the store. Which cat is guilty? The criminal does not wear glasses, is wearing a hat, and has more than three patches on their clothes.

BLOCKS

Look closely at each picture. Which cat has all the different kinds of blocks?

Finish drawing the houses below, then color them in.

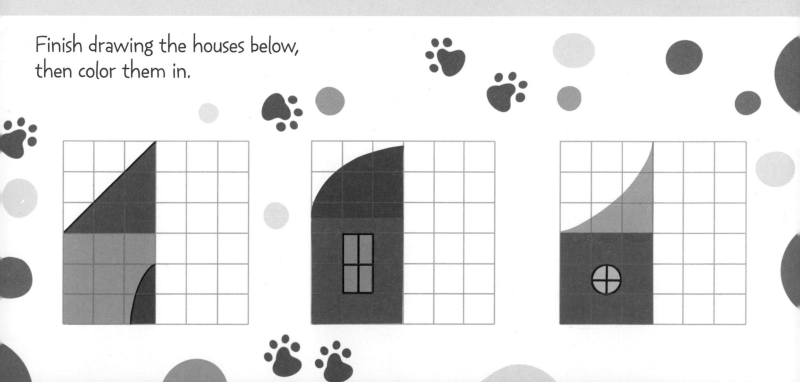

MISSING COLORS

There are colors missing from this page. Trace the lines from each object to see what color it should be. Then use crayons or markers to color the object in.

TiME TO PLAY!

Trace the dotted lines to find out who is playing with each ball of yard. Which cat doesn't have a ball of yarn?

SQUIRREL

SMOKY

MIA

Look at the patterns of beads below. Then follow each pattern to draw the rest of the beads to fill the string.

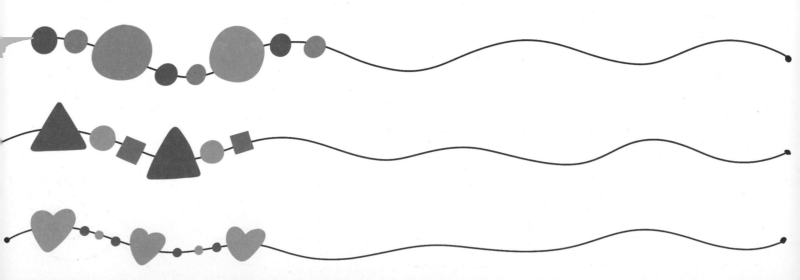

BATH TIME

Charlie has made a mess! Look at the key below. Can you find the seven objects in the bigger picture? Circle them.

I'M HUNGRY!

Oscar went for a long walk, and now he's tired and hungry! Help the sausage truck find the way to Oscar to give him a snack. Watch out for logs on the path!

OSCAR

START

WORLD'S FINEST SAUSAGES

LOST KEY

Oh, no! Detective Milo has lost his key in this mess! Look at the picture of the key next to him. Then find a path to it.

RUN, LITTLE MOUSE!

Help the mouse through the maze to get back to its house. Look at the key below to see which direction to move. Don't forget to collect the cookies, cheese, and apple, but watch out for the cats!

FINISH

2→ 1↓ 2→ 2↓ 2← 1↑
3← 2↓ 3→ 2↓ 1→

CONCERT

Look at the small pictures. Can you find them in the bigger picture? Which two are NOT in the bigger picture?

MOM, WHERE ARE YOU?

These kittens have gotten lost!
Help them find their way back
to their moms.

STUCK!

Toffee climbed the curtain, and now she's stuck! Help her find her way back down to the chair as quickly as possible.

TOFFEE

FINISH

FIND THE DIFFERENCES

Look carefully at these two pictures. Can you find 21 differences between them? Circle them as you find them.

OUTER SPACE

Jean wants to fly through space to the planet Burger. Can you help her find her way? Watch out for the pizzas and sausages that are blocking some of the paths!

FINISH

JEAN

MILK

POOLSIDE

Spice, Sugar, and Ember love milkshakes!
Look at the key below each cat to see which ingredients
are needed to make her favorite kind. Then trace the paths
to collect the items.

START

Marvelous
Milkshakes

SPICE

SUGAR

EMBER

VACATION SWIM

Joe went out for a swim, but now he wants to go back home. Can you help him find his way? Be sure to collect the red flags, and count the objects you see and write the numbers in the boxes.

JOE

FINISH

TAKE A WALK

Ollie wants to visit the big island with the cat statue, but he has to stop at all of the other islands first. Can you help him get through quickly?

OLLIE

FINISH

café

fish
ice cream

LUNCH TIME

These cats like different things. Follow the paths from each cat to find out what each one is having for lunch.

Each toy mouse is missing something. Figure out what it is, then draw the missing parts.

IN SPACE

Use the squares to help this feline astronaut draw
the rest of the rocket, then color it in.

TV TiME

Shadow's favorite TV show is on. But his friends Misty, Tiger, and Pudding have made a big mess in the room! Can you help Shadow find a path to the television?

Tweet tweet!

MISTY

TIGER

PUDDING

SHADOW

ESCAPE!

Ash does not like taking a bath!
Help him step on the tiles in the correct color
to get out of the bathroom.

FINISH

ASH

START

DAIRY PLANT

Brownie is thirsty! Can you find the path of pipes that will bring milk to his bowl? Then see if you can find two birds that are almost the same, but are different in one way.

START MILK

BROWNIE

COOKiES!

Help Star find a way through the cookie maze to Max. Make sure to collect all the cookies on the way!

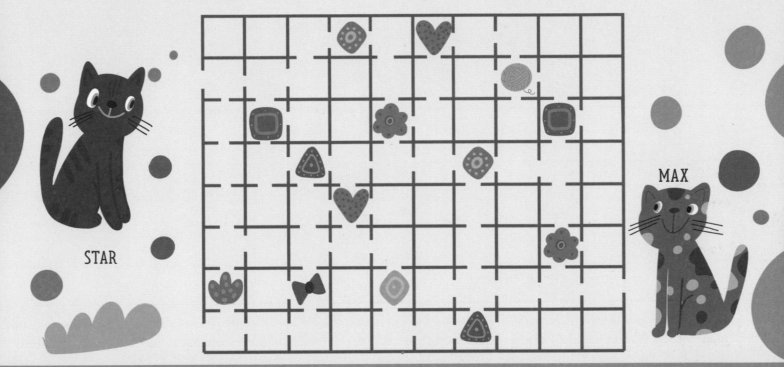

STAR

MAX

Start at the green dot and follow the directions to draw the picture. Who is it?

7↑ 1↗ 3→ 1↘ 2↓ 1↙
1← 1↙ 2↓ 1↙ 6← 1↗
2↑ 1↖ 1↗ 2↖ 2↗ 2↑
3↘ 3↓ 1↘

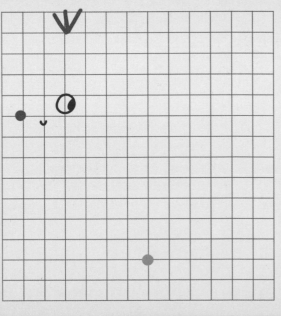

GET THE APPLES

Help the girl collect the apples that have
fallen from the tree.
Remember, you have to finish
where you started!

FINISH

START

ICE-CREAM CHAOS!

Uh-oh! There's ice cream spilling all over! Help Jannie find a path through the sticky mess so she can turn off the machine. Don't step in any of the pink ice cream!

FINISH

JANNIE

WHERE IS THE STONE?

All of these necklaces have fake stones in them, but only one also has a real stone. Can you help Detective Milo find the necklace with the real stone? Look at the key below, then follow the correct path.

FAKE STONES

LUNCHTIME!

Each kitten has a favorite food. Follow the lines to see who likes what.

GONE FISHING

Midnight, Snowball, Fluffy, and Peach are fishing, but only one of them caught a fish. Can you follow the fishing lines to figure out who it is?

Find the fish who make these shadows:

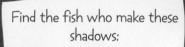